W9-BDJ-636

PENGUIN POCKET GUIDES

NEW ZEALAND'S
NATURE BIRDS

of Bush
and Countryside

PENGUIN BOOKS

Published by the Penguin Group
Penguin Group (NZ), 67 Apollo Drive, Rosedale, North Shore 0632
New Zealand (a division of Pearson New Zealand Ltd)
Penguin Books Ltd, Registered Offices: 80 Strand,
London, WC2R 0RL, England

First published in 1996
19 20

Text copyright © Penguin Books (NZ) Ltd 1996

Photographs © those people and organisations identified alongside
the reproductions

All rights reserved. Without limiting the rights under copyright
reserved above, no part of this publication may be reproduced,
stored in or introduced into a retrieval system, or transmitted, in any
form or by any means (electronic, mechanical, photocopying, recording
or otherwise), without the prior written permission of both the
copyright owner and the above publisher of this book.

Typeset by TTS Jazz, Auckland
Printed in Hong Kong through Asia Pacific Offset Ltd

ISBN-10: 0-14-026010-2
ISBN-13: 978-0-14-026010-6

CONTENTS

PENGUIN POCKET GUIDES

NEW ZEALAND'S
NATIVE BIRDS
of Bush
and Countryside

Text by
Ralph Powlesland

In association with Department of Conservation

ACKNOWLEDGEMENTS

Photographs in this book are the work of the following. The publisher wishes to acknowledge their expertise and assistance: **Brian Chudleigh:** front cover, pp. 2/3, 5, 14, 21, 22, 26, 27, 30, 32, 34, 37, 41, 46, 50, 53, 55; **Department of Conservation:** 10, 17, 19, 24, 25, 33, 36, 38, 44, 47, 54, 57, 59, 60, back cover; **Don Hadden:** 1, 8, 15, 16, 20, 23, 28, 31, 35, 39, 40, 42, 48, 49, 52, 56, 58; **Keylight Photo Library:** 18, 45, 51; **Craig Potton:** 12/13, 29, 43.

USING THIS BOOK

This **Penguin Pocket Guide to New Zealand's Native Birds** is an illustrated guide to the native and endemic birds of our bush and open country areas, of the offshore and outlying islands as well as the three main islands. The order in which subjects appear has been determined alphabetically by common name rather than by the more usual scientific classification of animal groups, the intention being to provide a work that can be more readily used by the general reader. A note on the scientific classification of the species herein appears on pages 62-3.

The size of each species, given at the end of the descriptive text, represents its length from the tip of its bill to the base of its tail. If not otherwise noted, the description of a species, including its size, is the same for both sexes.

The status of each species — that is, whether it is endemic or native — is based upon the following definitions:

Endemic — the species breeds in the wild *only* in the New Zealand region.

Native — the species breeds in the wild in the New Zealand region but *also* in other places outside this region.

INTRODUCTION

In prehistoric times, New Zealand was part of a single great land mass, the southern supercontinent of Gondwanaland. Its subsequent, unique environment was the result of long isolation from other land masses following the region's separation from Gondwanaland 80-60 million years ago.

This drift away from the larger land mass occurred after its colonisation by amphibians, reptiles and birds, but before the southwards dispersal of mammals to the Australasian region. So, free from browsing and predatory mammals, and isolated by the sea, New Zealand's plant and animal life evolved a special and unique character.

Primeval forest trees and plants that had died out in other larger lands continued to flourish here. Some of the birds became flightless and ground-dwelling, and adapted themselves to ecological niches that would elsewhere in the world have been filled by mammals. During the interglacial periods, low-lying areas were invaded by the rising seas and the higher land became islands. Isolated on these, many new species and subspecies evolved.

The impact, first of Polynesian settlers to New Zealand 1200 years ago, and then Europeans, just two centuries ago, had a disastrous impact on many of the habitats of its fauna, particularly those of birds. The burning and clearing of the forested lands coupled with the ravages of animal introductions caused a massive decline in bird numbers. During the nineteenth century the draining of swamps, the burning off of bush cover, and browsing by deer and

possum impacted on animal habitats, while predators like the stoat and feral cat caused untold damage to native bird populations, especially those of ground-dwelling species.

Continuing pastoral, forestry and industrial development this century has seen native habitats further reduced. In fact, many of the remnants of New Zealand's avifauna have been eliminated from the mainland altogether and are to be found only on offshore and outlying islands. Some of these islands remain almost wholly unmodified by settlement and have provided last bastions for species extinct on the mainland, as well as sanctuaries for transferred populations of endangered mainland species.

Some ten per cent of the world's endangered bird species are from the New Zealand region. The challenge of saving this unique wildlife is the responsibility of the Department of Conservation whose conservation projects, particularly those involving endangered bird populations, are world-renowned. The conservation of New Zealand's endangered species and the protection of their habitats will continue to be a major priority for the years ahead.

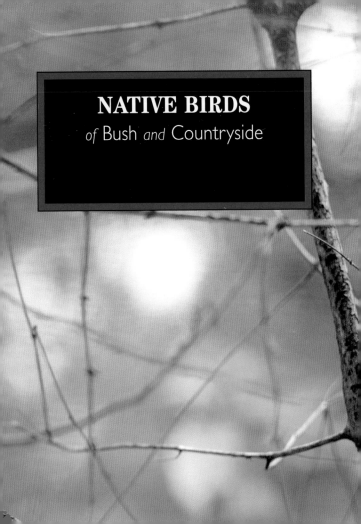

NATIVE BIRDS
of Bush *and* Countryside

Don Hadden

BELLBIRD (korimako)

BELLBIRD (Anthornis melanura)

This member of the 'honeyeaters' family feeds largely on nectar and berries. As a consequence, like several other native birds, it is responsible for the pollination of many native flowering plants. The bellbird's tongue, like that of other nectar-feeders such as the tui, is specially developed with 'brush' ends that are used to collect the nectar inside flowers. Named for the bell-like quality of its song, the bellbird is present in a wide range of habitats including home gardens and town parks as well as native forest. The female bellbird shares a similar plumage to the male but has none of the purple gloss and is generally duller in appearance compared with the male. The male of the species is slightly larger. There are three subspecies; the **New Zealand bellbird** (A. m. melanura) — occurring on the three main islands, on many of the offshore islands and at the Auckland Islands; the **Three Kings bellbird** (A. m. obscura) which is slightly larger than the mainland subspecies and is less yellow in its colouring, and the **Poor Knights bellbird** (A. m. oneho) of which the male has an iridescent blue head colour, compared with the violet iridescence of the other subspecies. (20 cm)
ENDEMIC

Don Hadden

BROWN CREEPER (pipipi)

BROWN CREEPER (*Mohoua novaeseelandiae*)

Like others of the warbler family, the brown creeper lives and feeds in the canopy of the forest and consequently is not often seen. It is, however, widespread throughout its range (the South Island, Stewart Island and some adjacent islands). The brown creeper is frequently observed in association with other species such as silvereyes, fantails and grey warblers with which it often flocks. Its cup-shaped nest is made using moss, leaves and strips of bark, and lined with grass and feathers. The brown creeper forages for insects along the branches and in the foliage of the canopy, often hanging upside down in this pursuit, a habit shared by other relatives such as the whitehead. Though common in native bush it is also present in pine forests. In the South Island it is the brown creeper that is the main host bird to the long-tailed cuckoo. (13 cm)

ENDEMIC

LONG-TAILED CUCKOO (koekoea)

DOC/J. Kendrick

LONG-TAILED CUCKOO (*Eudynamys taitensis*)

As with many other cuckoos in other parts of the world, the long-tailed cuckoo lays its eggs in the nests of other birds, leaving the rearing of the fledgling cuckoo to its 'hosts'. In the main the nests parasitised by this cuckoo are those of whiteheads, yellowheads and brown creepers. The long-tailed cuckoo is mostly insectivorous but will also feed on small lizards, and on birds' eggs and their young. Generally a solitary bird, it is distributed throughout the three main islands and on some offshore and outlying islands where it is found in native bush and pine plantations alike. At summer's end the cuckoo heads north to its wintering grounds on Pacific islands ranging from the New Hebrides east to the Marquesas Islands, from the Cook Islands north to the Ellice Islands. On Raoul Island in the Kermadec Islands group the long-tailed cuckoo is present all year round. It arrives in New Zealand in October each year. (40 cm)

ENDEMIC

Keylight/B. Enting

SHINING CUCKOO (pipiwharauroa)

SHINING CUCKOO (*Chrysococcyx lucidus lucidus*)

This small bird — slightly larger than a sparrow — is a distinctively coloured species displaying metallic green on its upper surface and boldly barred underparts. During the breeding season it is widespread in the three main islands and on some outlying islands. At the end of summer shining cuckoos migrate to the Solomon Islands and Bismarck Archipelago in the northwest Pacific. However, the occasional bird over-winters in New Zealand. Like the long-tailed cuckoo, the shining cuckoo does not build its own nest nor raise its young. Instead it lays its eggs in the nests of the grey warbler, whose own eggs and nestlings are pushed out of the nest or trampled: the young cuckoo is the sole survivor to be raised by its host parents. The cuckoo is found in both native and pine forest, in some farmland areas and even some suburban gardens. It feeds on insects. (16 cm)

ENDEMIC

NZ FALCON (karearea)

DOC/B. Harcourt

NEW ZEALAND FALCON (*Falco novaeseelandiae*)

This endemic species is distinguished from the harrier (p. 22) by its smaller size and darker colouring. As well, it flies with a faster wingbeat. Sexes share a generally similar plumage but with the female displaying less blue shading on the crown and nape, slightly darker underparts, and, sometimes, the absence of barring on the back. The falcon's nest is a scrape on the bare ground under a rock ledge or under a fallen branch, or is made among large epiphytes high in mature forest. The falcon mainly hunts birds but also preys on small lizards, insects and, occasionally, rabbits. It is distributed through both the two main islands and some offshore islands, preferring open country but often also nesting in forested areas. It is most abundant in the South Island, especially in the back country. (45 cm; female larger)

ENDEMIC

Don Hadden

Brian Chudleigh

NZ FANTAIL (piwakawaka)

NEW ZEALAND FANTAIL (*Rhipidura fuliginosa*)

Three subspecies of the New Zealand fantail occur, with both the North Island and South Island races being dimorphic. The great majority of the **North Island fantail** (*R. f. placabilis*) population are of the pied colour phase, but about a quarter of the **South Island fantails** occur as the dark phase (*R. f. fuliginosa*) — see opposite. All **Chatham Island fantails** (*R. f. penita*) are pied. Common to forest, park and garden habitats, fantails are instantly recognisable by their flitting, darting flight as they hawk their insect prey while on the wing, and by the attractive spreading tail. During the breeding season pairs of fantails will raise three or four broods in cup-shaped nests formed from moss, twigs and grass, and which are lined with fibres. The fantail's adaptation to human settlement has ensured a steady population. (16 cm)

NATIVE

AUSTRALASIAN HARRIER (kahu)

Brian Chudleigh

AUSTRALASIAN HARRIER *(Circus approximans)*

Also commonly known by the name 'hawk', the harrier is well distributed throughout New Zealand. Plumage is variable in colour but is generally dark brown on the upperparts, a lighter brown with dark banding on the tail, and reddish-brown with dark streaking on the underparts. The female is slightly larger than the male and shows more yellow-brown on the underparts. When flying, the harrier is readily identified by its slow effortless flight that alternates strong, deep flapping with soaring. Its wings form a shallow V as it circles in search of small mammals such as rabbits and hedgehogs, and rodents, insects and birds, including nestlings of forest species such as the New Zealand pigeon. Pastoral development has aided the harrier's expansion, as has the abundance of car-killed possums and rabbits on rural roads, on which the harrier gladly feeds. Its nest is often in swampland, sometimes in scrub and fernland, and usually on or near the ground. (60 cm; female slightly larger)

NATIVE

DOC/R. Morris

Don Hadden

KAKA (kaka-kura)

KAKA (*Nestor meridionalis*)

Two subspecies of this endemic parrot have evolved, one in each of the two main islands, where they inhabit heavily forested areas. The **North Island kaka** (*N. m. septentrionalis*) is also found on some offshore islands while the **South Island kaka** (*N. m. meridionalis*) also occurs on Stewart Island and a number of offshore islands. The South Island kaka differs from the North Island subspecies in having a generally more vivid plumage, but the most obvious distinction between the two subspecies is the almost white feathering of the South Island kaka's forehead and crown compared with the grey of the North Island kaka. Kakas live on fruit, nectar, sap and insects, and can be seen using their massive beaks to tear away rotten or live wood in search of insect larvae. Nests are made in hollow trees. Populations on the main islands are in decline as a result of predators such as stoats and rats which take eggs, chicks and sometimes even adult birds. (45 cm)

ENDEMIC

Original kakapo territory in Fiordland.

DOC

DOC/D. Merton

KAKAPO (tarapo)

KAKAPO (Strigops habroptilus)

Only 50 or so of this beautiful endemic parrot remain. Formerly widespread through forested areas of the North and South Islands, the kakapo has suffered severely from predation by introduced mammals such as rats and the stoat, and today its distribution is limited to transferred populations on Little Barrier, Maud and Codfish Islands. Its flightlessness and ground-nesting habit have meant that this bird is particularly vulnerable. A nocturnal species, the kakapo spends the day roosting in burrows, under thick cover or up in a tree. Although unable to fly, the kakapo, using its strong feet and beak, is able to climb trees to eat their fruits, its favoured diet. Other foods include roots, rhizomes and bulbs dug up with its beak. A characteristic habit is the systems of tracks and bowl-like depressions created by male birds, usually formed on a hill or ridge top. During some summers, the males gather at these track systems, spending much of each night giving a characteristic booming call in order to attract females for mating. The female alone incubates the eggs and raises the chicks. The kakapo is the world's heaviest parrot. (63 cm; female smaller)
ENDEMIC

Brian Chudleigh

KEA

KEA *(Nestor notabilis)*

A bird of the South Island mountain regions, the kea — its name derived from the bird's noisy call of *kea-a* — is most abundant on the western side of the Southern Alps. Its diet is similar to that of its relative the kaka but the kea is also something of a scavenger and can frequently be found around human habitations in search of scraps. The male is larger than the female and has a longer bill. Nesting begins in winter when much of the habitat is covered in snow, the nest often made in rock crevices. The kea is distinguished from the kaka (p. 23) by a brighter green plumage on its head, back and wings. (46 cm; female smaller)

ENDEMIC

NZ KINGFISHER (kotare)

NEW ZEALAND KINGFISHER
(*Halcyon sancta vagans*)

Frequently seen perched high up on a post-top or power line from where it is able to spot its prey, the kingfisher is a common sight in a wide range of habitats, from coastal open country and estuaries to lake shores, forests and farmland. Its readily identifiable staccato call of *kek-kek-kek-kek* is most commonly heard from spring to mid summer. Nests are made in holes dug into rotting trees and clay banks. Its diet comprises insects, small fish and birds, mice, earthworms and lizards. The kingfisher is distributed throughout the three main islands, and on numerous offshore islands. (24 cm)

ENDEMIC

BROWN KIWI (rowi)

Don Hadden

BROWN KIWI (*Apteryx australis*)

Three subspecies of the brown kiwi inhabit different areas of New Zealand and are distinguished by differences in colour and size. Kiwis are nocturnal, wandering about at night probing with their long bills for invertebrates in the litter, soil and in rotten logs. In addition, the diet of this and the other two species of kiwi includes seeds, berries and even freshwater crayfish. By day kiwis roost in burrows or thick undergrowth. The females of all three subspecies are larger and have longer bills than their male counterparts. The declining availability of suitable habitat and the predation of this ground-dwelling, flightless bird by stoats, ferrets and dogs means that the brown kiwi is under threat in much of its distribution.

Plumage of the **North Island brown kiwi** (*A. a. mantelli*) is mainly dark reddish brown streaked with black, especially on the back but with less of the tinting on the head. On average, the North Island brown kiwi is smaller than the other subspecies and is further distinguished by plumage that is coarser to the touch. This subspecies inhabits forest and scrub areas of the northern half of the North Island and is particularly

Craig Potton

numerous in forested areas of Northland. The male North Island brown kiwi alone incubates the clutch of one or two eggs, but the males of the other two subspecies are assisted by their mates, generally the females taking over at night while the males forage. The **South Island brown kiwi** (*A. a. australis*) is similar in colouring to the North Island brown kiwi but the streaking is a lighter, duller brown. It inhabits high-rainfall forests of South Westland and Fiordland. **The Stewart Island brown kiwi** (*A. a. lawryi*) has a greyer plumage than the other two subspecies and is the largest. It is found in forest, scrub and tussock habitats of the main island of the Stewart Islands group — Stewart Island — only. (50 cm)

ENDEMIC

GREAT SPOTTED KIWI (roa) – *and opposite*

GREAT SPOTTED KIWI (*Apteryx haastii*)

Larger than the little spotted kiwi, this species has a grey plumage which is distinctly mottled and barred brown-black. As for the other kiwi species, the call of the male is a high-pitched whistle, while the female's is a lower, harsh *churr*. Distribution is mainly West Coast South Island, from Okarito to northwest Nelson. The great spotted kiwi occurs in a wide range of habitats that includes rainforest, scrub and tussockland. (50 cm)

LITTLE SPOTTED KIWI (*Apteryx owenii*)

Once found on the West Coast of the South Island and in the southern part of the North Island, this species is now on the endangered list. The smallest and rarest of the kiwis, the total population of this species numbers about 1000 birds, most of which are to be found on Kapiti Island. As well as this population, transfers of birds have resulted in small but increasing populations on Long, Tiritiri Matangi, Hen, and Red Mercury Islands. It is distinguished from the great spotted kiwi by its smaller size and lighter colouring. (40 cm; female larger)
ENDEMIC

DOC/C.Veitch

KOKAKO

KOKAKO (Callaeas cinerea)

This is a bird of dense native forest, where it moves around in the canopy by running and hopping along branches with any flying more likely to be in the form of gliding between trees; the kokako has a weak flight and sustained flapping is uncommon. Insects, berries and leaves form the major part of its diet. Two races have evolved, the **North Island kokako** (*C. c. wilsoni*) and the **South Island kokako** (*C .c. cinerea*) that are differentiated by blue wattles in the case of the North Island subspecies, and orange wattles with blue bases in the case of the South Island subspecies. The kokako is now rare, with the South Island race almost extinct. Introduced mammalian predators and competitors have caused major declines in the distribution of the North Island kokako in recent years, especially in Northland and Taranaki. However, recent transfers of birds to Little Barrier and Kapiti Islands have established small populations at these places. In addition, determined efforts by the Department of Conservation that have reduced numbers of predators and competitors to very low levels in central North Island reserves have resulted in notable increases in kokako numbers there. (38 cm)
ENDEMIC

Don Hadden

MOREPORK (ruru)

MOREPORK *(Ninox novaeseelandiae)*

Distinguished from the little owl, an introduced species, by its larger size and darker colouring, the morepork is found throughout New Zealand. It has generally adapted successfully to settlement and its characteristic call of *more-pork* can be heard from urban parks and reserves, pine plantations and even suburban gardens, in addition to its natural habitat of native bush. A nocturnal bird, the owl is insectivorous in the main but hunts small mammals also. During the day it roosts in dense vegetation, or inside a cave or hollow tree. Nests are usually in hollow trees, but may also be found in thick clumps of epiphytes and in holes in banks. (29 cm)

ENDEMIC

RED-CROWNED PARAKEET (kakariki)

DOC/C. Veitch

RED-CROWNED PARAKEET
(*Cyanoramphus novaezelandiae*)

Four subspecies occur, all sharing a red forehead and crown, a red band from forehead to eye and a red patch behind each eye. The **red-crowned parakeet** (*C. n. novaezelandiae*) was formerly widely distributed throughout the North and South Islands but is now present in only small numbers in those regions. It is, however, populous on many offshore and outlying islands. The **Kermadec parakeet** (*C. n. cyanurus*) shows a greater amount of blue on its wings and on its tail while the **Chatham Island red-crowned parakeet** (*C. n. chathamensis*) has more emerald-green on the face and yellower underparts. The latter is distributed on a number of islands in the Chatham group and sometimes breeds with the **Forbes' parakeet**, a union that results in birds that have orange-edged, or wholly orange crowns. Occurring only on Antipodes and Bollons Islands the **Reischek's parakeet** (*C. n. hochstetteri*) has distinctive, more yellow-green plumage above and below and its crown and eye-stripe and patch are orange-red rather than crimson red. (28 cm; female smaller)
ENDEMIC

Brian Chudleigh

YELLOW-CROWNED PARAKEET (kakariki)

YELLOW-CROWNED PARAKEET
(*Cyanoramphus auriceps*)

There are two subspecies: one, the **yellow-crowned parakeet** (*C. a. auriceps*), is found in large native forests in the North and South Islands, as well as Stewart Island and many offshore and outlying islands; the other, the **Forbes' parakeet** (*C. a. forbesi*) of the Chatham Islands. A very rare subspecies, the Forbes' parakeet differs from the mainland race in its larger size and in the crimson frontal band which is narrower and does not fully reach the eye. Previously considered a separate species, the rare orange-fronted parakeet is now considered to be a colour variant of the yellow-crowned parakeet. The orange-fronted form is found at a few localised areas of the South Island, often in association with yellow-crowns. The orange form has an orange frontal band and a paler orange stripe from the forehead to the eyes. The diet of the yellow-crowned parakeet is similar to that of its red-crowned cousin, namely tree buds, shoots, flowers, leaves and seeds, as well as insects. (26 cm; female smaller)

ENDEMIC

DOC/J. Kendrick

ANTIPODES ISLAND PARAKEET

ANTIPODES ISLAND PARAKEET
(Cyanoramphus unicolor)

Larger in size than other parakeets, this species is readily identified by its entirely green head and face that is without frontal bands or eye stripes. It also differs in nesting in burrows or on the ground under shelter of thick vegetation, like tussock or sedge. Distribution is limited to the Antipodes and Bollons Islands plus a number of adjacent islets in the Antipodes Island group. (31 cm; female smaller)

ENDEMIC

Don Hadden

NZ PIGEON (kereru)

NEW ZEALAND PIGEON
(*Hemiphaga novaeseelandiae*)

There are two subspecies of the New Zealand pigeon. The more common **New Zealand pigeon** (*H. n. novaeseelandiae*) is found throughout the lowland native forests of the three main islands and a number of offshore islands, while the **Chatham Islands pigeon** (*H. n. chathamensis*) is found only on islands in the Chatham group where it replaces the New Zealand pigeon. The Chatham Islands race is larger than the mainland race and further distinguished by its more robust beak and having grey flight feathers and rump. Once abundant in the Chatham group, it is now rare, numbering about 150 birds. The mainland race has adapted to a variety of habitats and even occurs in some urban areas where pockets of native bush provide both food and nesting sites. The pigeon is a herbivorous feeder, eating the fruits, berries, leaves and flowers of native trees — the miro is especially favoured — and some exotic trees and shrubs. It breeds mainly in the late spring and summer when fruit is available, a single white egg being laid on a platform of twigs. (51 cm)
ENDEMIC

Don Hadden

NZ PIPIT (pihoihoi)

NEW ZEALAND PIPIT (*Anthus novaeseelandiae*)

Often confused with the skylark, the pipit shares a similar colouring and shape and is often seen in many of the same habitats. However the pipit is a more slender bird, lacks the skylark's head crest, and when on the ground frequently gives its tail a characteristic flick up and down. The pipit occupies open country from the coast to the mountains, including rougher farmland. It builds its nest on the ground, a cup-shaped construction that is usually well hidden in long grass or scrubby groundcover. Several subspecies occur: the **New Zealand pipit** (*A. n. novaeseelandiae*); the **Antipodes Island pipit** (*A. n. steindachneri*); the **Chatham Island pipit** (*A. n. chathamensis*), and the **Auckland Island pipit** (*A. n. aucklandicus*). The upper parts of the New Zealand subspecies are various shades of brown and it has a distinctive white eyebrow streak. By comparison the Auckland Island pipit has yellow-brown plumage. The Antipodes Island pipit is an even duller yellow-brown. The Chatham Island pipit has the palest plumage of the four subspecies. Insects comprise the main part of the pipit's diet but earthworms, snails, seeds and berries are also taken. (19 cm)
ENDEMIC

Brian Chudleigh

SPUR-WING PLOVER

SPUR-WINGED PLOVER
(*Vanellus miles novaehollandiae*)

Self-introduced from Australia, the spur-winged plover has been breeding here since the 1930s. From an initial pair of birds that arrived in Southland the spur-winged plover is now distributed throughout the country. Although it prefers wettish pastoral sites, the plover can be seen over most lowland open habitats such as cultivated paddocks, stubble, riverbeds, estuaries and even sandy beaches. Flocks of hundreds of birds are not uncommon in the autumn and winter when plovers congregate. Its diet consists of invertebrates, particularly caterpillars and earthworms. Named for the small (10 mm-long) wing spurs that protrude from the wings at each shoulder, this plover is also readily identified by its colouring of brown-above and white-below and its yellow bill and face wattles. (38 cm)

NATIVE

Don Hadden

RIFLEMAN (titipounamu)

RIFLEMAN *(Acanthisitta chloris)*

The rifleman is a bird of the forest interior and today is found mainly in larger remnant native forests. Two subspecies occur, the **North Island rifleman** (*A. c. granti*) and the **South Island rifleman** (*A. c. chloris*). The former is distributed on Little and Great Barrier Islands in addition to central and southern North Island while the South Island subspecies is found throughout the South Island and on Stewart and Codfish Islands. Both races share a similar colouring and are distinguishable from the rock wren by their wholly white underparts. The sexes have distinguishing plumage, males being green above while females are brown. Nests are made in holes in tree trunks, or earth banks, and in thick tangles of vegetation such as the hanging dead leaves of cabbage trees and the fronds of tree-ferns. Its diet is wholly insectivorous, including a wide variety of flies, spiders, caterpillars and moths which the rifleman collects from the trunks and branches of trees. (8 cm)

ENDEMIC

Craig Potton

ROBIN (toutouwai) – *South Island robin, male*

ROBIN *(Petroica australis)*

Characterised by dark grey upperparts, a white chest and an upright stance on long legs, the three subspecies of robin are familiar inhabitants of the New Zealand forest. In some areas it can now also be found in pine plantations, especially those of the central plateau of the North Island. The robin mainly frequents the forest floor where it hunts insects, grubs and worms. Large prey items are broken up and some portions cached for eating later the same day or the following one. The robin is a noted songster, males occasionally singing loudly for over 30 minutes. Robins have a patch of white feathers at the base of the beak which are usually hidden, but are flashed at other species, such as fantails, before chasing them from an area. Nesting robins suffer high losses of eggs, chicks and even adult females to introduced predators.

The **North Island robin** (*P. a. longipes*) is largely confined to the forests of the central North Island and to Little Barrier and Kapiti Islands. Colouring is dark grey-brown, with an irregularly shaped patch of white on the breast and belly. The female is generally browner and lighter in colour than the male. The male **South Island robin** (*P. a.*

South Island robin, female

Don Hadden

australis) displays a darker upper surface and more extensive yellow-tinged white breast and belly than its North Island cousin. The female is browner above and has a lesser degree of yellow underneath. *P. a. australis* is widely dispersed through the South Island with much apparently suitable habitat being unoccupied. The **Stewart Island robin** (*P .a. rakiura*) is similar in appearance to the South Island robin but slightly smaller, darker on the upper surface and has whiter underparts. This race is present only on Stewart Island and a few of its outliers. (18 cm)

ENDEMIC

DOC

Keylight/Brian Chudleigh

CHATHAM ISLAND BLACK ROBIN

CHATHAM ISLAND BLACK ROBIN

(*Petroica traversi*)

One of the world's rarest bird species, the black robin had a population of just seven birds in the mid-1970s before the start of a Wildlife Service programme of transfer and cross-fostering that has saved this bird from extinction, increased its numbers substantially and created two strong populations on Mangere Island and South East Island in the Chatham group. It was formerly widespread on a few islands in the Chathams but predation by cats had reduced the population to less than 50 by the turn of the century. Those remaining, on Little Mangere Island, were faced with a deteriorating and diminishing habitat. A reafforestation programme on the bigger Mangere Island preceded their transfer there. The black robin's nest is usually made in hollows in trees or old stumps. Like the mainland robins, it will sometimes make use of an abandoned blackbird's nest, the robin simply relining the cup-shaped base. The population of black robins in now more than 100. (15 cm)

ENDEMIC

SADDLEBACK (tieke) – *North Island saddleback*

Brian Chudleigh

SADDLEBACK *(Philesturnus carunculatus)*

Named for the bright chestnut saddle over its wings and back, the saddleback is also distinguished by the characteristic orange wattles at the base of its bill. The saddleback is a bird of the forest and dense scrub, and nests in holes in trees or under cover of heavy vegetation. Foraging from the forest floor to the canopy it feeds on insects and grubs prised out from the rotten wood of dead branches and from under the bark of trees, as well as fruits. The **North Island saddleback** (*P. c. rufusater*) is identified by a narrow yellow-buff band along the front edge of the saddle. The **South Island saddleback** (*P. c. carunculatus*) lacks the band and has smaller wattles, but otherwise adults have a similar plumage to the North Island race. Juveniles of *P. c. rufusater* are similar in colouring to their parents — although lacking the yellowish band — but South Island saddleback juveniles are a uniform reddish-brown. One of the endemic family of New Zealand wattlebirds that includes the kokako and the now extinct huia, the saddleback is an endangered species formerly widespread through the North and South Islands but now reduced to remnant populations on offshore islands. Distribution of the North Island saddleback comprises Hen Island and transferred

North Island saddleback

DOC/C. Veitch

populations on several other offshore islands including Red Mercury and Kapiti. The South Island saddleback is found on a small number on islets off Stewart Island, and there are transferred populations on Breaksea and Motuara Islands. (25 cm; female of both subspecies slightly smaller)

DOC/C. Veitch

ENDEMIC

Don Hadden

SILVEREYE (tauhou)

SILVEREYE (Zosterops lateralis)

Also commonly known as 'whiteye' and 'waxeye' for the distinctive white ring marking around the eye, this colonist was self-introduced from Australia in the 1830s. It began breeding in New Zealand in the 1860s and in the years since it has spread to all parts of the country, including the Chatham Islands and the subantarctic island groups. It has adapted well to settlement and is common in home gardens as well as native forest, scrub and orchards. The silvereye forages for a wide variety of foods, taking, in addition to a natural diet of fruit, nectar and insects, handouts of bread and fat. Its nest is a finely worked cup-shaped construction that is hung off slender branches. Hair, moss, cobwebs and grass are all used in the making of the nest. (12 cm)

NATIVE

Don Hadden

STITCHBIRD (hihi) – *male*

STITCHBIRD (*Notiomystis cincta*)

Formerly common throughout the North Island and on a number of offshore islands, the stitchbird has been extinct on the mainland since late last century and its main population is now confined to Little Barrier Island. Small transferred populations also exist on Kapiti Island, and Mokoia Island in Lake Rotorua. The stitchbird is another of the 'honeyeater' family and its diet is largely nectar extracted with its brush-tipped tongue from the flowers of native plants such as flax, rewarewa, pohutukawa and kohekohe. Like other nectar-eating birds the stitchbird is an important pollinator in the forests it inhabits. It also eats fruit and insects. The stitchbird is sexually dimorphic, males being larger and more colourful (black head, neck and breast, white ear tufts, and yellow on wings and lower margin of black breast) than females (mainly olive brown above). Nests are made in holes in the trunks and branches of its forest habitat. Recent research has established that the stitchbird is New Zealand's only known polygynandrous breeding bird, whereby two or more males and two or more females nest together. (19 cm)
ENDEMIC

Brian Chudleigh

Female stitchbird

WELCOME SWALLOW

Brian Chudleigh

WELCOME SWALLOW (*Hirundo tahitica*)

Until the late 1950s the welcome swallow was a rare visitor to this country from Australia but subsequently it has established itself widely, to the extent that it is now common in many parts of New Zealand and on some outlying islands. The swallow is an inhabitant of open country near water where it feeds on insects taken on the wing. Characteristic is its swift, low, swooping, darting flight. Nests are mud and grass cups attached to vertical surfaces mainly under bridges, in culverts, and occasionally on and in buildings and caves. Flocking is frequent from midsummer through to early spring when such flocks break up for breeding. (15 cm)

NATIVE

Keylight/B. Enting

TAKAHE (moho)

TAKAHE *(Porphyrio mantelli)*

Considered extinct for much of this century, the takahe was dramatically rediscovered in 1948 in the Murchison Mountains west of Lake Te Anau. Today the takahe is still known from the Murchison and the adjoining Stuart Mountains in the Fiordland National Park, where it maintains a tenuous foothold. A population of less than 200 individuals faces the dual threat of a low reproductive rate (just a single nesting each year, only two eggs on average in the clutch and a high chick mortality) and competition and predation from introduced animals. The takahe feeds on the succulent leaf bases of tussocks and a mountain daisy and the seeds of various tussocks and grasses. In winter, when snow blankets the grasslands and prevents feeding, the takahe retreats into the adjoining beech forest to feed on herbs and the nutritious rhizomes of the summer-green fern. Superficially similar to the pukeko, the takahe is more robust and has shorter, thicker legs. Head, neck, breast and flanks are an iridescent turquoise, and the legs, frontal shield and massive bill, bright red. Small transferred populations have been established on a small number of offshore islands. (63 cm)
ENDEMIC

Don Hadden

NZ TOMTIT (piropiro) – *South Island tomtit, male*

NEW ZEALAND TOMTIT (*Petroica macrocephala*)

Insectivorous feeders, taking insects from the forest floor to the canopy, and off foliage and branches, the five subspecies of tomtit are found in both native and exotic forest and shrub. They are separated from the related robins by a greater expanse of white or cream colouring on the breast and abdomen — in all except the Snares Island tomtit — a more horizontal stance, and smaller size. Except for the Snares Island tomtit, which is entirely black, the plumage of male tomtits is black above with pale or yellow-white underparts. Females are more greyish- or olive-brown above and have buff streaking on the underparts. The South Island tomtit differs from the North Island subspecies in that the breast immediately below the black of the neck is orange for a few millimetres, shading into yellow, which becomes very pale at the lower belly. These colours are most intense following the moult in autumn, and often become quite pale by spring. The male plumages of the Chatham Island tomtit and Auckland Island tomtit are similar to that of the South Island tomtit. The **North Island tomtit** (*P. m. toitoi*) is found throughout the North Island and on a number of offshore islands, while the range of **South Island tomtit** (*P. m. macrocephala*) comprises the South Island,

Brian Chudleigh

Chatham Island tomtit, male

Stewart Island and a number of offshore islands. The **Chatham Island tomtit** (*P. m. chathamensis*) shows a black-on-white patterning with an orange or red tinge on the breast and while it is no longer present on Chatham Island this subspecies is well established in residual forest and scrub on other islands in the group. The **Auckland Island tomtit** (*P. m. marrineri*) occurs on Auckland Island and five other nearby islands. The **Snares Island tomtit** (*P. m. dannefaerdi*) occurs on the main island and one other. (13 cm)

ENDEMIC

DOC/C. Veitch

TUI

TUI (*Prosthemadera novaeseelandiae*)

A bird of native forest and, in the northern half of the North Island in particular, of bush reserves and bush remnants in suburban areas, the tui is identified by its swooping, undulating flight and flash of white wing-bar. The tuft of white feathers at its throat may also be visible. The tui is another of the endemic honeyeaters and feeds mainly on nectar — from flowers of native plants such as kowhai and flax — but fruits and insects are eaten as well. Its fluid, melodious song — sometimes confused with that of the bellbird — combines bell-like notes with harsh clicks, barks, cackles and wheezes. Two subspecies occur; the **New Zealand tui** (*P. n. novaeseelandiae*) — distributed throughout the three main islands and on many offshore and outlying islands — and the **Chatham Island tui** (*P. n. chathamensis*) which is distinguished from the former by its longer throat feathers and the deeper blue of its chest plumage. (30 cm; female smaller)

ENDEMIC

Brian Chudleigh

GREY WARBLER (riroriro)

GREY WARBLER (*Gerygone igata*)

The grey warbler's sustained trilling song is a familiar one both in the bush and in suburban habitats throughout New Zealand. The nest of the **grey warbler** is an elongated pear-shaped construction hung from branches and often secured at the sides and base as well. The nest is enclosed, with access given by a small circular hole on one of the sides. The warbler is the main host to the shining cuckoo; it is the warbler's second clutch that is parasitised. The warbler is insectivorous, catching caterpillars in particular. Pairs of birds tend to remain together outside the breeding season but can be seen through autumn and winter in flocks mixed with fantails, brown creepers, silvereyes and other species. A separate species, the **Chatham Island warbler** (*G. albofrontata*), occurs on Chatham Island and on a number of the outliers in the group. It is a larger bird than the mainland race and has a more contrasting plumage, being mainly olive-brown above and white below. (11 cm)

ENDEMIC

WEKA – *Western weka*

Don Hadden

WEKA (*Gallirallus australis*)

Four subspecies of this large flightless bird occur on the three main islands as well as a number of offshore islands. The weka is generally of a brown-black colouring and ranges over a variety of habitats from coastline to swamp and river flats, scrub country and mountain bush. It walks with deliberate steps accompanied by tail flicking and is characteristically inquisitive: birds readily investigate human activity in their territory — as trampers well know. The weka is omnivorous, feeding by day and night on fallen fruit, seeds, invertebrates, lizards, snails, the eggs and young of birds, and small rodents. Its distribution has gradually diminished in some areas, particularly in the North Island, mainly as the result of the removal of thick scrub cover adjacent to farmland and the predations of introduced mammalian predators, particularly dogs.

The **buff weka** (*G. a. hectori*) formerly inhabited the eastern districts of the main range of the South Island but is now confined to Chatham Island and Pitt Island to which it was introduced in the early 1900s. Re-introduction of the species into Canterbury from the Chathams has

Brian Chudleigh

North Island weka

been unsuccessful to date. It has a lighter overall colouring than the other races. The **western weka** (*G. a. australis*) is to be found mainly in the northern and western regions of the South Island from Nelson to Fiordland. Distinguished by dark red-brown and black streaking on the breast, the western weka has two distinct colour phases, that of the southernmost range showing a greater degree of black. The **Stewart Island weka** (*G. a. scotti*) is smaller than the other subspecies and, like the western race, has two colour phases; a chestnut form — similar to the chestnut-phase western weka — and a black phase which is not as dark as the black western weka. The population is confined to Stewart Island and outliers, and to Kapiti Island to which it was introduced. The **North Island weka** (*G. a. greyi*) is represented by original populations in Northland and Poverty Bay, and by liberations elsewhere from that stock. This subspecies differs in its greyer underparts, and brown rather than reddish coloured legs. (53 cm)

ENDEMIC

Don Hadden

WHITEHEAD (popokatea)

WHITEHEAD (*Mohoua albicilla*)

The whitehead hunts insects in the leafy canopy of the forest and from under the bark of trunks and branches. It eats seeds and fruits as well. Inhabiting both exotic pine forests and native forests the whitehead is the main host in the North Island to the long-tailed cuckoo, which not only parasitises the whitehead's nest but also preys on its eggs and young. The female whitehead is slightly smaller than the male and is differentiated by a brown wash over the white crown and nape. Flocking occurs in the autumn. Found mostly in the southern half of the North Island, the whitehead also occurs on Kapiti, Little Barrier and Great Barrier Islands, and as an introduced population on Tiritiri Matangi Island. (15 cm)

ENDEMIC

ROCK WREN

ROCK WREN (Xenicus gilviventris)

Found above the bushline on the rockfields and scree slopes of the central mountain ranges of the South Island, the rock wren hunts for insects and spiders among the rocks, and nests in the crevices between them. It has large feet to help it cling to its rocky habitat and is characterised by a bobbing and bowing habit. Colouring is olive-brown above (the male generally brighter than the female) with dark green tail feathers. Rock wrens of the southernmost range, in Fiordland, are a brighter green on top and display more yellow on the flanks. This population is considered by some observers to be a separate subspecies, *X. g. rineyi.* (9.5 cm)

ENDEMIC

YELLOWHEAD (mohoua)

DOC/D. Geddes

YELLOWHEAD (*Mohoua ochrocephala*)

Formerly widespread throughout the South Island and Stewart Island, the yellowhead is now confined mainly to the larger tracts of native forest in the lower South Island. Wetas, spiders, beetles, caterpillars and other insects comprise the main part of the yellowhead's diet, but it eats fruit as well. Nests are made in holes in trees or stumps. Sexes have a similar appearance, the female, however, showing a duller yellow on its head and underparts. This bird is another that is parasitised by the long-tailed cuckoo. (15 cm)

ENDEMIC

SCIENTIFIC CLASSIFICATION

All animals and plants are grouped and classified according to their structure, shape, physiology, distribution and mode of life. In this way relationships between groups of living things can be established.

The basic single natural unit in this classification system is the *species*, a group whose members in the wild can interbreed and produce fertile offspring. Closely related species form a *genus*. Related genera form *families*, and families *orders*. Orders are grouped into *classes*, classes into *phyla*, and phyla are grouped into either the animal or plant kingdoms. In giving a species its scientific classification, a generic name, representing the name of a group of related species (or genus), is followed by the specific name of the particular species. The names are in Latin, and the two together are known as the species' scientific name. In the case of a subspecies, a third or trinomial name follows the specific name.

A subspecies occurs where part of the population within a species shows distinct differences in appearance — in size, shape or colour. Subspecies, or races, usually also occupy a distinct geographical area, often as isolated populations on islands where they have evolved in isolation from other groups of the same species. In New Zealand with its numerous offshore and outlying islands and steep, confining, mountainous terrain, a considerable number of subspecies have evolved.

In the following list, the bird species presented in this book are grouped by their scientific classification, the families and orders of families appearing in the conventional sequence of most ancient through to most evolved.

| **ORDER** | **APTERYGIFORMES — *Kiwis*** |
| FAMILY | APTERYGIDAE — *Kiwis* |

| **ORDER** | **FALCONIFORMES — *Hawks, falcons and vultures*** |
| FAMILY | ACCIPITRIDAE — *Eagles, hawks and allies;* **Australasian harrier** |

FAMILY	FALCONIDAE — *Falcons*, **New Zealand falcon**

ORDER	**GRUIFORMES — *Cranes, rails and allies***
FAMILY	RALLIDAE — *Rails;* **takahe, weka**

ORDER	**CHARADRIIFORMES — *Waders and gulls***
FAMILY	CHARADRIIDAE —*Lapwings, plovers and dotterels;* **spur-winged plover**

ORDER	**COLUMBIFORMES — *Pigeons and doves***
FAMILY	COLUMBIDAE — *Pigeons and doves;* **NZ Pigeon**

ORDER	**PSITTACIDAE — *Cockatoos and parrots***
FAMILY	CACATUIDAE — *Cockatoo;* **kakapo**
FAMILY	NESTORIDAE — *New Zealand parrots;* **kaka, kea**
FAMILY	PLATYCERCIDAE — *Broad-billed parrots;* **parakeet**

ORDER	**CUCULIFORMES — *Cuckoos and turacos***
FAMILY	CUCULIDAE — *Cuckoos, koels and coucals;* **long-tailed cuckoo, shining cuckoo**

ORDER	**STRIGIFORMES — *Owls***
FAMILY	STRIGIDAE — *Owls;* **morepork**

ORDER	**CORACIIFORMES — *Kingfishers, rollers and allies***
FAMILY	ALCEDINIDAE — *Kingfishers;* **New Zealand kingfisher**

ORDER	**PASSERIFORMES — *Perching birds***
FAMILY	XENICIDAE — *New Zealand wrens;* **rifleman, New Zealand rock wren**
FAMILY	HIRUNDINIDAE — *Swallows and martins;* **welcome swallow**
FAMILY	MOTACILLIDAE — *Pipits and wagtails;* **NZ Pipit**
FAMILY	MUSCICAPIDAE — *Flycatchers, warblers, thrushes and allies;* **brown creeper, fantail, robin, black robin, tomtit, grey warbler, whitehead, yellowhead**
FAMILY	ZOSTEROPIDAE — *Silvereyes*
FAMILY	MELIPHAGIDAE — *Honeyeaters;* **bellbird, stitchbird, tui**
FAMILY	CALLAEIDAE — *New Zealand wattlebirds;* **kokako, saddleback**

INDEX